Helping at Mealtime

by Brienna Rossiter

www.focusreaders.com

Focus Readers is distributed by North Star Editions:
sales@northstareditions.com | 888-417-0195

Produced for Focus Readers by Red Line Editorial.

Photographs ©: Shutterstock Images, cover, 1, 4, 7, 8, 10, 13, 14, 16, 18, 20

Library of Congress Cataloging-in-Publication Data
Names: Rossiter, Brienna, author.
Title: Helping at mealtime / by Brienna Rossiter.
Description: Lake Elmo, MN : Focus Readers, 2021. | Series: Spreading
   kindness | Includes index. | Audience: Grades 2-3
Identifiers: LCCN 2020033616 (print) | LCCN 2020033617 (ebook) | ISBN
   9781644936849 (hardcover) | ISBN 9781644937204 (paperback) | ISBN
   9781644937921 (pdf) | ISBN 9781644937563 (ebook)
Subjects: LCSH: Dinners and dining--Juvenile literature. | Helping
   behavior--Juvenile literature. | Kindness--Juvenile literature.
Classification: LCC TX737 .R68 2021 (print) | LCC TX737 (ebook) | DDC
   641.5/4--dc23
LC record available at https://lccn.loc.gov/2020033616
LC ebook record available at https://lccn.loc.gov/2020033617

Printed in the United States of America
Mankato, MN
012021

About the Author

Brienna Rossiter is a writer and editor who lives in Minnesota. She loves cooking food and being outside.

Table of Contents

Chapter 1

You Can Help

People often make meals for their friends and family. Making food for others is one way to show that you care for them.

Ask the person who is **preparing** the food what you can do to help. You could wash or peel vegetables. You could **measure** the **ingredients**. Or you could help mix them.

Chapter 2

Getting Ready

Before a meal, you can help
set the table. First, set one
place for each person. Put
out dishes and napkins. Next,
add **utensils**.

Then, think about what **condiments** people might need. Bring them to the table. When the food is ready, you can bring it to the table, too.

Fun Fact For fancy meals, people may fold napkins into shapes such as animals or flowers.

Set the Table

There are many ways to set the table. Try using this simple way! The plate goes in the middle. A napkin goes to the left. Place a fork next to the napkin. Put a spoon and knife on the right side of the plate. A glass goes above the spoon and knife.

Place Setting

Chapter 3

At the Table

When it's time to eat, pass the food around the table. You can hold dishes for others or help serve food. You can pour drinks for others, too.

If you don't like how something tastes, don't make a face. And don't say it tastes bad. You could hurt the cook's feelings. Instead, thank the person for making the food.

Fun Fact

In some countries, burping is rude. But in other places, it tells the cook you loved the food.

Chapter 4

Cleaning Up

After eating, you can help clean up. Take your dishes to the sink. Offer to take other people's dishes, too. You can help put away **leftover** food.

You can also help clean the dishes. Wash them or put them in the dishwasher.

Later, help dry the dishes or put them away. That way, the kitchen is ready for the next meal.

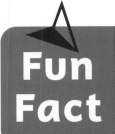

Fun Fact

A dishwasher gets very hot inside. It can melt some kinds of plastic.

Helping at Mealtime

Write your answers on a separate piece of paper.

1. Write a sentence describing one way to help prepare food.

2. Would you rather help make food or help clean up after a meal? Why?

3. What should you do if something tastes bad?
   A. make a face
   B. say it tastes bad
   C. thank the person who made it

4. How does helping to clean up after a meal show kindness?
   A. It leaves less work for the person who made the food.
   B. It makes more work for the person who made the food.
   C. It leaves more space on the table.

Answer key on page 24.

Glossary

condiments
Things that add flavor to food. Salt, pepper, and ketchup are common condiments.

ingredients
Foods that are mixed together to make a meal.

leftover
Extra or unused.

measure
To find the amount of something.

preparing
Making something ready to be used.

utensils
Tools that people use to eat. Forks, spoons, knives, and chopsticks are common utensils.

To Learn More

BOOKS

Huddleston, Emma. *Cooking a Meal.* Lake Elmo, MN: Focus Readers, 2021.

Plattner, Josh. *Manners at Mealtime.* Minneapolis: Abdo Publishing, 2016.

NOTE TO EDUCATORS

Visit **www.focusreaders.com** to find lesson plans, activities, links, and other resources related to this title.

Index

Answer Key: 1. Answers will vary; 2. Answers will vary; 3. C; 4. A